THIS IS YOUR SPIRITUAL RETREAT

THIS IS YOUR SPIRITUAL RETREAT

A Journal for
Cultivating Your Potential

CHRONICLE BOOKS
SAN FRANCISCO

BRIAN LEAF   MATT OESTREICHER

ISBN: 978-1-7972-0975-3

Manufactured in China.

MIX
Paper from
responsible sources
FSC™ C008047

Design by Rachel Harrell.

10 9 8 7 6 5 4 3 2 1

Chronicle books and gifts are available at special quantity
discounts to corporations, professional associations, literacy programs,
and other organizations. For details and discount information,
please contact our premiums department at
corporatesales@chroniclebooks.com or at 1-800-759-0190.

Chronicle Books LLC
680 Second Street
San Francisco, California 94107
www.chroniclebooks.com

To Benji, Noah, and Hannah

TABLE OF CONTENTS

HOW TO USE THIS BOOK

CONGRATULATIONS! YOU'RE HOLDING THIS BOOK, AND
THAT MEANS SOMETHING. IT MEANS YOU'RE READY FOR
THIS ADVENTURE. IT MEANS THAT YOU WANT MORE: MORE
COMFORT. MORE JOY IN YOUR RELATIONSHIPS AT HOME OR AT
WORK. MORE CLARITY IN YOUR LIFE'S PURPOSE. A CLARIFIED
CONNECTION TO SPIRIT. YOU'RE READY FOR YOUR OWN
PERSONAL SPIRITUAL RETREAT.

During this retreat you'll identify which habits and patterns in your life are holding you back, discover ways to move past the blocks and challenges, and find a new, higher level of well-being.

This isn't the kind of retreat that requires you to leave your life behind or puts a huge dent in your savings. You can continue working, parenting, exercising, gardening, praying, or partying—whatever you ordinarily do in your day-to-day life. This retreat is nondenominational and helpful to everyone. You don't need to seclude yourself on a mountaintop to find wisdom. The wisdom is here, and you've taken the first step to unlocking it and changing your life.

Your retreat consists of eighteen prompts and activities. You can take your time and spread the eighteen prompts over the course of six months, or you can complete all of them quickly in just a few weeks. What matters most is mindful participation. Commit to the work in the eighteen prompts, and you'll experience the transformation that you've signed up for.

As you work through the prompts, we recommend keeping this book with you throughout your day—in your backpack, purse, briefcase, gym bag, or yoga bag—as a reminder that you are on a retreat, even as you continue going about your life. Use the book as a talisman to look at or hold when you need inspiration or resolve to stay focused on the process.

Some of the prompts will direct you to this website for additional resources: www.thisisyourspiritualretreat.com. And, of course, if ever you need more room for any of the prompts in this book, feel free to use a notebook or blank journal.

And now it's time. You're ready for your spiritual retreat. Proceed to Prompt 1.

ONE

What Brought You Here?

Welcome, once again, to *This Is Your Spiritual Retreat.* And congratulations, you've made it here!

Let's start at the

very beginning.

To get somewhere on this journey, you must clarify your intention for it. Answer each of the following questions, filling in all the lines. The more detailed you can be in your answers, the more likely you are to get what you need from the retreat. Be as specific as you can.

How was your day today? What did you do so far today?

_____

_____

_____

_____

_____

_____

_____

_____

_____

_____

How or why did you select this book? Why are you seeking a spiritual retreat?

_____

_____

_____

_____

_____

_____

_____

_____

_____

_____

_____

_____

_____

_____

_____

_____

_____

_____

_____

_____

_____

_____

_____

_____

_____

_____

_____

_____

What are you looking for in your life? What are you needing most
right now?

_____

_____

_____

_____

_____

_____

_____

_____

TWO

I, _____,
NAME

am entering into my own personal spiritual

retreat on this day, the _____ of _____
DATE   MONTH

in _____. I intend to complete the eighteen prompts of
YEAR

This Is Your Spiritual Retreat. I may experience moments of

joy, clarity, peace, and insight, as well as moments of discom-

fort and fear, but I intend to see the retreat through and know

that I will emerge wiser and happier, with new skills and tools

for greater well-being, a clarified sense of my life's purpose,

and a deeper connection to spirit.

_____
SIGNATURE

The Contract

Sometimes while on a retreat, we can experience great joy and boosted energy and vitality. Other times, we may find ourselves facing difficult feelings or uncomfortable realizations.

> *And, of course, we always finish*
> *with new tools and a deeper*
> *understanding of ourselves.*

To make sure we get to that point, it helps to make a commitment to finish the retreat, to see it through. It also helps to have a ritual that officially begins the retreat. Fill out the contract on page 17 as that opening ritual and to solidify your commitment to finishing it.

Make your contract a symbol of your commitment to completing this retreat, your own personal North Star to steer you forward and keep your resolve strong, regardless of the calm, choppy, or even tempestuous seas you experience in any given moment.

After you've completed the contract, carefully remove the page from this book. Decorate it; make it beautiful. Then find a frame (or sketch one around your contract), and place your framed contract in a special space, somewhere you'll see it every day. Put it on your dresser, near the bathroom mirror, on the wall, even on an altar if you want. An altar can simply be a space to put objects that hold a special meaning for you.

Your altar can be something as simple as a shoebox or a crate, or as fancy as a beautiful mahogany stand.

Adorn it with special stones, statues, or objects from nature, such as pine cones.

THREE

Your Memoir

Before we know where to go,

we need to know where we are now

and where we have been.

On the following pages, write a memoir describing each year of your life, using only one or two sentences per year. For example, if you're fifty years old, you'll write fifty to one hundred sentences. Make a numbered list and then fill in a sentence or two next to each number.

How can one reduce a full year into one or two sentences? Surprise yourself by writing the first thing that comes to mind. What impression do you have of that year? What do you remember? What challenges were you dealing with that year? What feelings were the most prominent? Don't just write a biography of facts or a list of events. Go deeper.

After you're done, go directly to Prompt 4. Don't reread what you've written. There will be time and space to review it later.

PROMPT

FOUR

NUMBER

Memoir Review

Answer the questions in these three prompts, in order, on the following pages.

A.   How do you feel now, after writing your memoir and before rereading it? What thoughts or feelings have come up for you while writing? Do you have any reflections or insights? Record them below:

_____

_____

_____

_____

_____

_____

_____

_____

_____

_____

_____

_____

_____

_____

_____

_____

B.   After you've journaled about your initial reflections, go back
     and reread your memoir. This part is key: Notice any themes
     that emerge as you reread it. In other words, what patterns,
     repeated difficulties, or recurring dramas do you notice?
     What threads show up throughout the memoir? Record your
     observations.

_____

_____

_____

_____

_____

_____

_____

_____

_____

_____

_____

_____

_____

_____

_____

_____

C.   Are the themes you found while rereading your memoir what you expected? Did anything surprise you?

Some people find that many sentences are about wanting more love in their life. Some find that many are about money fears, or wanting to pursue a certain interest or passion. Others find that in many sentences, they're blaming someone (a boss, a parent, a teacher) for their pain. Some see a lot of success in a certain aspect of life (like business or dating), are surprised by repeated mentions of success in a sport, or find more of a focus on music than they expected.

Record your observations below:

_____

_____

_____

_____

_____

_____

_____

_____

_____

_____

_____

_____

FIVE

Home Spa Break

Introspection can be challenging work, and the mind and body can best digest and integrate changes when relaxed, so self-care and some pampering are vital parts of this home retreat.

Today your task is to take a load off:

rest, relax, and treat yourself.

Choose an item or two from the menu on the following pages to create your own home spa break. Whichever items you choose, drink lots of fresh water throughout the day.

Choose an item or two from the menu below:

- *Create a spa in your own bathroom. Light a few candles. Use bath salts or bubble bath if you want. Use incense if you like. Play some relaxing music. (You can find meditation music at www.thisisyourspiritualretreat.com.) Relax.*

- *Put on some music and move your body. Dance it out! Let loose. Don't hold back. Dance your true self.*

- *Start a journal. Decorate the cover. Make it sacred.*

- *Try the simple Mindful Self-Massage practice in the Appendix (page 142). It relieves stress and promotes healthy circulation. You can also download the guided Mindful Self-Massage practice at www.thisisyourspirtualretreat.com.*

- *Take a walk in a gorgeous location (the woods, the desert, along a river, on the beach) and be especially mindful of the scenery. If possible, stay there until your mind settles and you can truly see the scene.*

- *Take an online yoga class. We recommend restorative yoga, which involves passive stretches held for a long time, often supported by props, such as blankets or blocks.*

- *Have a walk or tea with a beloved friend or family member, someone who makes you feel safe and supported.*

- *Try a deep, deep yoga nidra (guided yogic relaxation). Yoga nidra aims for a profound level of relaxation in a state between waking and sleep, which is deeply restorative. You can download the guided relaxation at www.thisisyourspirtualretreat.com.*

SIX

Finding the Core Insight

Look back at your journal entries from Prompt 4. Pay attention to the themes, patterns, repeated difficulties, recurring dramas, and trends that you wrote about. As you do so, watch your feelings and reactions. Which theme or pattern feels the most ripe and charged? Which one feels important to work on?

Write about it here:

_____

_____

_____

_____

_____

_____

_____

_____

_____

_____

_____

_____

_____

_____

_____

_____

_____

_____

_____

_____

_____

_____

_____

_____

Capture that theme, pattern, repeated difficulty, recurring drama, or trend in a concise sentence or two. Let's call this your core insight.

MY CORE INSIGHT IS:

SEVEN

Energy-Building Practices

Before we decide what to do about the core insight you noticed in your memoir, it's helpful to boost your energy level. Each of the following practices is simple yet has great power to clear your mind, charge your energy level, and bring insight, all of which can allow you to break old mental or emotional habits and achieve new growth.

Choose one or two items from the following list and dedicate yourself to that practice for the next five days. Choose a practice that you're not already doing daily. And again, whichever practice you choose, drink lots of fresh water.

- Eat more veggies, especially dark leafy greens.

- Cut refined sugar from your diet.

- Experiment with a vegan diet.

- Before each meal, while seated at the table, close your eyes, feel your feet on the ground, and relax your body. Take three slow, deep breaths, smell your food, and give thanks for your meal.

- Enjoy a daily thirty-minute walk in the woods or desert, or on the beach.

- Take a daily twenty-minute jog followed by ten minutes of simple stretching.

- Create art for fifteen or more minutes per day.

- Do a daily mindfulness meditation (see Prompt 9, page 64).

- Relax with ten minutes of gentle stretching every morning and every night.

- Dedicate time every day to connecting with beloved friends or family.

- Spend an hour each day in silence, and then spend one full day in silence, being quiet and introspective. If you live with people, carry a notebook to communicate, if needed.

- Find a way to be of service part of each day for five days. Volunteer daily at a soup kitchen or shelter, participate in Best Buddies or Big Brothers/Big Sisters, or join a volunteer organization or board. Donate food to a local food pantry, or clothes or unneeded goods.

- Attend a spiritual or religious service. It can be one you grew up with or something totally new to you.

- Plan a session to seek counsel with a coach, therapist, minister, or religious leader. Journal each day about what you'll seek from your session.

- Attempt radical honesty. No lies (even little tiny ones).

- Do at least twenty minutes of yoga postures followed by ten minutes of guided relaxation daily. You can find a local class at a yoga center or gym, or try an online class.

Place your commitment (following page) on your altar or somewhere where you'll see it every day: above your bed, on your bathroom mirror, or maybe in your planner. You can even take a photo of it and make it the home screen on your laptop or phone.

_____
DATE

I, _____,
                 NAME

will commit for the next five days to _____

_____

_____

_____

_____

_____

                    _____
                              SIGNATURE

During these five days of commitment, spend a few minutes each day journaling about the practice you chose. Answer the following questions:

Is the practice easy or difficult to follow?

Do you notice any changes in your mood, energy level, creativity, or morale?

Day 1:   Date _____

_____

_____

_____

_____

_____

_____

_____

_____

_____

_____

_____

_____

_____

_____

_____

_____

Day 2:   Date _____

_____

_____

_____

_____

_____

_____

_____

_____

_____

_____

_____

_____

_____

_____

_____

_____

_____

_____

Day 3:   Date _____

_____

_____

_____

_____

_____

_____

_____

_____

_____

_____

_____

_____

_____

_____

_____

_____

_____

_____

_____

_____

_____

_____

_____

Day 4:   Date _____

Day 5:   Date _____

_____

_____

_____

_____

_____

_____

_____

_____

_____

_____

_____

_____

_____

_____

_____

_____

_____

_____

_____

_____

_____

EIGHT

_____
DATE

I, _____,
                NAME

will commit for the next five days to _____

_____

_____

_____

_____

_____

_____
          SIGNATURE

Considering Your Core Insight

Choose a second item from the energy-building practices list in Prompt 7 and add it to your daily routine. Fill out the commitment on page 57.

For this prompt, think about your core insight from Prompt 6. Read your core insight a few times each day, perhaps in the morning before you do your energy-building practice, before you journal, and/or before bed. And, as you build vital energy this week, watch for any clarity or inspiration regarding your core insight.

As you did in Prompt 7, spend a few minutes during each of the five days journaling. Answer the questions:

Is the practice easy or difficult to follow?

Do you notice any changes in your mood, energy level, creativity, or morale?

Do you notice any clarity or inspiration regarding your core insight?

Journal on the following pages.

Day 1:   Date _____

_____

_____

_____

_____

_____

_____

_____

_____

Day 2:   Date _____

_____

_____

_____

_____

_____

_____

_____

_____

_____

_____

_____

_____

_____

_____

_____

_____

_____

_____

_____

Day 3:　　　　　　　　　　　　　　　　　　Date _____

_____

_____

_____

_____

_____

_____

_____

_____

_____

_____

_____

_____

_____

_____

_____

_____

_____

_____

_____

_____

_____

_____

Day 4:   Date _____

Day 5:   Date _____

_____

_____

_____

_____

_____

_____

_____

_____

_____

_____

_____

_____

_____

_____

_____

_____

_____

_____

_____

_____

_____

NINE

Mindfulness

You've applied self-discipline with directed effort to build your energy. Now we let it do its work. We surrender. It's like the glide after the stroke in swimming. Today, we sit still and meditate.

Start right now.

After you read this paragraph, sit up, alert but relaxed. Close your eyes and concentrate on your breath. Choose a point to focus on, either the rise and fall of your belly as you breathe or the air passing through your nostrils. To help you stay focused, count your breaths up to ten and then start again at one. Whether you are new to meditation or a seasoned master, your mind will likely wander. That's totally normal and expected. Whenever you notice that your mind has wandered, simply bring it back by counting your breaths.

Try this now for a few minutes, then journal on the following page.

NOTE: We've created a guided audio meditation you can download at www.thisisyourspiritualretreat.com.

How do you feel after focusing on your breath for a few minutes?

_____

_____

_____

_____

_____

_____

_____

_____

_____

_____

_____

_____

_____

_____

Meditation is a practice. As you continue to meditate, your ability to stay focused grows. And perhaps more importantly, your ability to forgive yourself and apply compassion when you notice that your mind has wandered also grows.

For the next seven days, starting today, reserve time for two five-minute meditations in your schedule every day. This can be first thing in the morning, in your car when you get to work, before lunch, or before bed—whatever works for you.

Journal in the space below after each meditation. Describe how the practice felt. Was it easy or hard? How did you feel afterward?

Day 1: Date _____

_____

_____

_____

_____

_____

_____

_____

_____

_____

_____

_____

_____

_____

_____

_____

_____

Day 2:   Date _____

_____

_____

_____

_____

_____

_____

_____

_____

_____

_____

_____

_____

_____

_____

_____

_____

_____

_____

_____

_____

Day 3:   Date _____

_____

_____

_____

_____

_____

_____

_____

_____

_____

_____

_____

_____

_____

_____

_____

_____

_____

_____

_____

_____

_____

Day 4:   Date _____

_____

_____

_____

_____

_____

_____

_____

_____

_____

_____

_____

_____

_____

_____

_____

_____

_____

_____

_____

Day 5:   Date _____

_____

_____

_____

_____

_____

_____

_____

_____

_____

_____

_____

_____

_____

_____

_____

_____

_____

_____

_____

_____

_____

Day 6:   Date _____

_____

_____

_____

_____

_____

_____

_____

_____

_____

_____

_____

_____

_____

_____

_____

_____

_____

_____

Day 7:   Date _____

TEN

Meditation for Clarity

What was your core insight from Prompt 6?

_____

_____

_____

_____

_____

_____

_____

Has your core insight shifted at all since then? If so, describe how below:

_____

_____

_____

_____

_____

_____

_____

_____

Meditation is like letting a snow globe settle so you can see the scene inside more clearly. And this clarity allows for new observations and insight into a situation. The insight can be a deeper understanding of what's really going on, a fresh idea or approach to a challenge or problem, a revelation about the nature of the situation, or even what feels like guidance from spirit.

This week, continue to practice two short meditations every day, just as you did in Prompt 9.

Meditate at whatever times

work best for you.

Sit up, alert but relaxed. Close your eyes and concentrate on your breath. Choose a point to focus on, either the rise and fall of your belly as you breathe or the air passing through your nostrils. To help you stay focused, count your breaths up to ten and then start again at one. Whenever you notice that your mind has wandered, simply bring it back by counting your breaths.

*Now we'll add one more piece
to the meditation. You've built
the energy, you've made an
intention to calm the mind, and
now you'll ask for inspiration.*

For the next seven days, starting today, set the intention to receive clarity, a deeper understanding, or guidance about your core insight, just as you did as you built the energy in Prompt 8. You don't have to force this. It's not an effort. Just meditate as before and simply open the door to inspiration. Count your breaths and wait for any insights to come. These kinds of repeated exercises and activities are some of the most powerful parts of this retreat. It's helpful to do it again, so come to the practice anew each time.

NOTE: Don't judge the clarity or guidance that comes. Don't worry about what it means or what to do with it. Just keep this book handy and write down any insights as they appear.

Each day after you meditate, journal on the following pages. Describe how the practice felt. Was it easy or hard? How did you feel afterward? And do you notice any new understanding, clarity, or guidance regarding your core insight?

Day 1:   Date _____

_____

_____

_____

_____

_____

_____

_____

_____

_____

_____

_____

_____

_____

_____

_____

_____

_____

_____

_____

_____

_____

Day 2:   Date _____

_____

_____

_____

_____

_____

_____

_____

_____

_____

_____

_____

_____

_____

_____

_____

_____

_____

_____

Day 3:   Date _____

_____

_____

_____

_____

_____

_____

_____

_____

_____

_____

_____

_____

_____

_____

_____

_____

_____

_____

_____

_____

_____

Day 4:   Date _____

_____

_____

_____

_____

_____

_____

_____

_____

_____

_____

_____

_____

_____

_____

_____

_____

_____

_____

Day 5:   Date _____

Day 6:   Date _____

_____

_____

_____

_____

_____

_____

_____

_____

_____

_____

_____

_____

_____

_____

_____

_____

_____

_____

_____

Day 7:   Date _____

ELEVEN

It's Time to Share

Sometimes keeping our challenges, feelings, or insights to ourselves lets them build momentum and power. And sometimes it's essential to share them with others.

You've probably had the experience of being sad or upset about something, but after sharing it with a friend, therapist, or loved one, being surprised by how much better you feel. Or gained understanding of a situation after simply saying it out loud to someone else. Or figured out the solution to an issue just as the words were leaving your lips.

Today, make a plan to share your core insight with a trusted person. Discuss any ways it's changed, along with the clarity or guidance you found in Prompt 10.

Make a short list of people with whom you can be vulnerable and feel safe sharing deeply.

_____

_____

_____

_____

_____

_____

_____

_____

_____

Who will you meet?

_____

_____

_____

_____

_____

When and where?

_____

_____

_____

_____

_____

_____

_____

_____

_____

_____

After you meet, journal below.

How did it go? What happened when you shared? How did you feel?

_____

_____

_____

_____

_____

_____

_____

_____

_____

_____

_____

_____

_____

_____

_____

_____

_____

What did you realize or learn about yourself from sharing?

_____

_____

_____

_____

_____

_____

_____

_____

_____

_____

_____

_____

_____

_____

_____

_____

_____

_____

Did you arrive at any new understanding of your core insight through sharing?

_____

_____

_____

_____

_____

_____

_____

_____

_____

_____

_____

_____

_____

_____

_____

_____

_____

_____

TWELVE

Resolve Your Core Insight

How has your understanding of your core insight from Prompt 6 evolved through energy-building practices, journaling, meditation, inspiration, and sharing with a trusted friend?

Describe below:

_____

_____

_____

_____

_____

_____

_____

_____

_____

_____

_____

_____

_____

_____

_____

_____

_____

_____

_____

_____

_____

If your core insight has shifted, write the updated version in a concise sentence or two here.

MY CORE INSIGHT IS:

Now we'll change your core insight statement into an I AM or an I HAVE statement. In other words, we'll shift your core insight statement into its resolution. If it was "I need" or "I am missing [something]," we'll change it to "I have" that something. If it was "I am bad at," it becomes "I am good at."

If your core insight is about what you lack, such as "I'm missing a loving relationship in my life," change it into something you have, such as "I have a loving relationship in my life."

If your core insight is that you wish you could be as happy as you were in college, your I AM statement is "I am deeply happy now."

If your core insight is that you've felt unloved, your I AM statement is "I am loved."

If your core insight is "I've always been ashamed of my body," then your I AM statement is "I am proud of my body."

If you notice that you've felt like a fraud at work, your I AM statement is "I am talented, respected, and successful at work."

If your core insight is that you need a better job, your I AM statement is "I have the perfect job."

Now we understand that you may think, *BUT wait, I am not loved*, or *BUT I don't have the perfect job*. That's OK. In this experiment, we're going to see what it feels like to have it.

Craft your I AM statement below. (And go for it! Write "I AM" and then all that you want in life!)

Draft and edit it here:

_____

_____

_____

_____

_____

_____

_____

_____

_____

_____

_____

_____

_____

_____

_____

_____

Once you have crafted your I AM statement, write the final version here:

PROMPT

THIRTEEN

Fake It Till You Make It

Reread your I AM statement. Say it out loud. How does it feel to say it? Does it succinctly capture all that you want in life regarding your core insight? If needed, edit it. Then write your new I AM statement in the box.

Edit it here, if necessary:

_____

_____

_____

_____

_____

I AM

Now—and here is the real key—after you read this paragraph, close your eyes and feel deeply that your I AM statement is true. It's fine to fake it. But really go for it. How do you feel when your I AM statement is true? How do you walk and hold yourself? Is your posture different? How do you interact with others? With whom do you have a different relationship? Feel that your I AM statement is true and hold that feeling/thought. Close your eyes and see it. Afterward, journal below.

How did you feel when you held your I AM statement as true?

_____

_____

_____

_____

_____

_____

_____

_____

_____

_____

_____

_____

_____

_____

What thoughts and feelings arose?

Your homework for Prompt 13 is to continue steeping in this I AM statement for the rest of today. Read it and think about it as often as you can. Embody it.

As you steep in your I AM statement, notice how you feel. Take a few notes below.

When I believe my I AM statement is true, I feel:

_____

_____

_____

_____

_____

_____

_____

_____

_____

_____

_____

_____

_____

_____

_____

PROMPT

FOUR
TEEN

Another Spa Break!

Time for some self-care and pampering. You've been doing powerful work, and getting relaxed will help your mind and body digest and integrate changes.

So today, let's again take a

load off. Rest and relax.

Choose an item or two from the menu on the following pages to create your own home spa break.

Here is the list of Spa Break choices again. Select one or two and treat yourself. You can repeat something you loved from the previous spa break and/or choose new ones this time:

- *Create a spa in your own bathroom. Light a few candles. Use bath salts or bubble bath if you want. Use incense if you like. Play some relaxing music. (You can find meditation music at www.thisisyourspiritualretreat.com.) Relax.*

- *Put on some music and move your body. Dance it out! Let loose. Don't hold back. Dance your true self.*

- *Start a journal. Decorate the cover. Make it sacred.*

- *Try the simple Mindful Self-Massage practice in the Appendix (page 139). It relieves stress and promotes healthy circulation. You can also download the guided Mindful Self-Massage practice at www.thisisyourspiritualretreat.com.*

- *Take a walk in a gorgeous location (the woods, the desert, along a river, on the beach) and be especially mindful of the scenery. If possible, stay there until your mind settles and you can truly see the scene.*

- *Take an online yoga class. We recommend restorative yoga, which involves passive stretches held for a long time, often supported by props, such as blankets or blocks.*

- *Spend some time with a beloved family member or friend, perhaps someone who makes you laugh.*

FIFTEEN

Testing Your I AM Statement

Once again, reread your I AM statement. Say it out loud. Does it succinctly capture all that you want in life regarding your core insight? Are you still happy with it, or do you need to tweak it? If needed, edit it below. Then write your new I AM statement in the box.

_____

_____

_____

_____

_____

_____

_____

_____

_____

_____

_____

_____

_____

_____

_____

_____

_____

_____

_____

_____

_____

_____

If you changed your I AM statement, write it below:

After you read this paragraph, as you did in Prompt 13, visualize that your I AM statement is true. How do you see yourself at home or work when you hold that this statement is true? How do you stand, move, dress, and groom yourself? What do you wear? How do you speak and what do you say? How do you interact with others? How do you spend your time? Close your eyes and visualize this again. These kinds of small, incremental changes in mental state are some of the most powerful parts of this retreat. It's helpful to do it again, so come to the practice anew each time.

What did you visualize? Describe below:

_____

_____

_____

_____

_____

_____

_____

_____

_____

_____

_____

_____

_____

_____

Now let's take your I AM statement out for a spin.

Go to a meeting, home to your roommates or partner and kids, to a nearby town where no one knows you—whatever you're comfortable with—and feel as though your I AM statement is true. Embody that feeling. Wear it. Be it. Remember, it's OK if, for now, you have to fake it.

Make a specific plan. Where and when will you go to take your I AM statement out for a spin?

Where:

_____

_____

_____

_____

_____

_____

_____

_____

_____

_____

_____

_____

_____

When:

_____

_____

_____

_____

_____

_____

_____

_____

_____

_____

How does this plan feel (e.g., scary, comfortable, exciting)?

_____

_____

_____

_____

_____

_____

_____

OK, you are ready. Take your I AM statement out into the world. You can do it. Then describe your experience below.

How did it feel? What happened? Was it easy? Difficult? Did any insights emerge?

_____

_____

_____

_____

_____

_____

_____

_____

_____

_____

_____

_____

_____

_____

_____

_____

_____

_____

_____

SIXTEEN

You Have Control

What resistance came up when you carried your I AM statement into your day? This might have been a voice that said, "You can't," or "This could never happen."

If you're not sure, try the visualization again:

After you read this, close your eyes and embody your I AM statement. As you embody I AM, do you have any thoughts or feelings of doubt that say, "No, you can't," or "I could never have that success"?

Write about that here:

_____

_____

_____

_____

_____

_____

_____

_____

_____

_____

_____

_____

_____

What does it feel like to believe that voice of resistance, to believe the opposite of the I AM statement? For the next few moments, embody it. Visualize the feeling of "You can't," or "This could never happen." Wear it and walk around in it.

How do you feel? Does your posture change? What do you feel in your body? Write about that experience here:

_____

_____

_____

_____

_____

_____

_____

_____

_____

_____

_____

_____

_____

_____

_____

_____

And now contrast it with how you feel when you hold that your I AM statement is true. Visualize it and walk around for a few moments as though it is true. How does that feel? What's the difference?

Switch back and forth a few times. Feel that your I AM statement is true. Then feel that it's false. Describe below how each one feels in your mind, emotions, and body. Does it change your stance or posture? Does it change your energy level, outlook, or mood?

_____

_____

_____

_____

_____

_____

_____

_____

_____

_____

_____

_____

_____

_____

_____

_____

Do any insights emerge from switching back and forth?

_____

_____

_____

_____

_____

_____

_____

_____

_____

_____

_____

_____

_____

_____

_____

_____

_____

_____

Notice that in this visualization, switching back and forth between embodying your I AM statement and rejecting it, you have some control over how you feel. You have control in how you carry yourself, how you show up in the world, and most importantly, how you feel about yourself, moment to moment.

That's the key.

You have control

over how you feel about yourself,

moment to moment.

Try it again.

Feel that your I AM statement is true. Then feel that it's false. Notice the difference.

All that changes between the two is how you choose to regard yourself. It's that simple. It's your choice.

Make a commitment right now to choose to feel that your I AM statement is true.

First say: "I hold my I AM statement as true." And then: "My I AM statement is true."

In fact, repeat your I AM statement aloud right now. Mean it. Hold it as true and notice how you feel.

Write your I AM statement again here:

*I AM*_____

Write your I AM statement on your home screen, set it as a reminder on your phone, or leave it written on notes for yourself in hidden places. Post it on your bathroom mirror or above your bed. Carry it in your wallet, purse, or backpack. Place it on your altar or on your desk in your office.

You get the idea—anything to help you remember.

And with that, my friend, you have almost graduated from this retreat.

You now have the power to decide how you feel.

Let that sink in.

SEVEN TEEN

Retreat Review

Describe the journey you've taken in your spiritual retreat through these past sixteen prompts.

_____

_____

_____

_____

_____

_____

_____

_____

_____

_____

_____

_____

_____

_____

_____

_____

_____

_____

_____

_____

_____

_____

What was easy and what was difficult on this journey?

_____

_____

_____

_____

_____

_____

_____

_____

_____

_____

_____

_____

_____

_____

In what ways have you grown and changed?

_____

_____

_____

_____

_____

_____

_____

_____

_____

_____

_____

What is the most important lesson you've learned?

_____

_____

_____

_____

_____

_____

What exercises, energy-building practices, spa breaks, or new habits from the retreat will you keep practicing?

_____

_____

_____

_____

_____

_____

_____

_____

_____

_____

_____

_____

_____

_____

_____

_____

Make a specific plan to continue these exercises, energy-building practices, spa breaks, or new habits. How will you do them? When?

_____

_____

_____

_____

_____

_____

_____

_____

_____

_____

_____

_____

_____

_____

_____

_____

_____

_____

Use the following pages to write a letter to your future self. Describe what you learned in your retreat. What do you want to reinforce or remind your future self? What questions do you have?

Carefully tear out the pages of your letter and seal them in an envelope. In the corner of the envelope, write a date that's four weeks from today. Put your letter in your sock drawer. Set a reminder on your calendar or phone for four weeks in the future, and on that date, open and read your letter to yourself.

Dear Self,

_____

_____

_____

_____

_____

_____

_____

_____

_____

_____

_____

_____

_____

_____

EIGHTEEN

This certificate is to acknowledge

that I,_____, have completed a
NAME

spiritual retreat on this day, the _____ of
DATE

_____ in _____ . I have completed the
MONTH   YEAR

eighteen prompts of *This Is Your Spiritual Retreat*. I experi-

enced moments of discomfort and fear, but saw it through to

emerge with new skills and tools for greater well-being. I am

grateful for _____ ! Great job, me!

_____
SIGNATURE

Completion

You did it! Congratulations!

It's important to mark the end of a retreat. To celebrate. To honor the work you've put in, the effort you've undertaken, and the growth you've experienced. Take some time to decorate and carefully cut out the certificate on the following page. You can frame it or post it somewhere where you'll see it every day.

Choose a place to keep the certificate. Imbue it with energy. Make the promise to yourself that every time you see it, you will reaffirm your commitment to embody your I AM statement.

Matt and I would like to say a personal congratulations. You've accomplished something important here. We're on the path together, and we'd love to hear from you at community@thisisyourspiritualretreat.com. Feel free to share anything about your experience with us or ask any questions that you may have.

Also, when the time feels right, you can do the retreat again. We love redoing the memoir experience. As we grow, the practice grows with us, ready to take us to the next level of well-being.

In peace, love, and celebration,

Brian and Matt

Acknowledgments

Thank you, thank you to our editors Deanne Katz and Leigh Saffold, to designer Rachel Harrell, and to illustrator Charlotte Ager. Thanks to so many teachers and mentors who inspired and shepherded us on the path: Swami Kripalu, Laighne Fanney, Yoganand Michael Carrol, Sudhir Jonathan Foust, Shobhan Richard Faulds, Probhakar Jeff Migdow. Gratitude to Gwen, Alyssa, Noah, Benji, and Hannah for time, love, and support. And lastly, many thanks to Mecha Noodle Bar and Shearwater Coffee in Fairfield, Connecticut, where we ate soup, drank coffee, explored our own core insights, and wrote the bulk of this book.

Appendix

MINDFUL SELF-MASSAGE

Think of this massage as a ritual where you're letting your body know it can relax, that it's being taken care of. Let your touch be guided by the intention of self-love. Don't worry about technique. You can use your thumbs or hands, or even tap your body with soft fists. As you do the massage, send thanks to your muscles for all the work they do in your life. Send healing energy through your hands to each body part. Spend at least 30 seconds on each part of your body, or more as needed and if time allows.

1. FEET: Sit on the floor with the soles of your feet facing each other and your knees out to the sides. Massage the bottom of each foot. Focus on the sensations in your feet.

2. LEGS: Hold the front of your shins with your fingers as you use your thumbs to gently work on your calves.

3. BACK: Straighten your legs in front of you. Reach behind to your lower back and use your fingertips to make small circles, pressing on both sides of the spine but not directly on the spine.

4. SHOULDERS: Reach your right hand across your chest to grab and massage the left side of your shoulder next to your neck. Switch to your left hand to massage your right shoulder. You can also grab the outside of each shoulder (deltoid) and squeeze it as if it was a tennis ball.

5. NECK: Use your thumbs to rub the sides and back of your neck.

6. ARMS: Use your right hand to rub up and down your left forearm, hand, and fingers. Switch and do the other arm.

7. FACE and HEAD: Place your palms over your eyes and gently rub your forehead and the top of your head. Then place your hand on the back of your head, with your fingers on top of your head, and use your thumbs to rub where the head and neck meet.

8. EARS: Gently massage your ears with your fingers.

9. Notice if there is any part of your body that you want to return to and give additional attention to.

10. Take a few moments to relax and soak in the effects of the self-massage.

11. Perhaps follow up with a rest, a nap, or a warm shower.

You can download audio instructions from www.thisisyourspiritualretreat.com.

About the Authors

Brian Leaf, MA, is the author of seventeen books, including *The Teacher Appears: 108 Prompts to Power Your Yoga Practice*, and *Misadventures of a Garden State Yogi*, as well as the *Be You Card Deck for Teens*, with coauthor Matt Oestreicher. Brian has a BA in business, English, and theology from Georgetown University and an MA from Lesley College, specializing in yoga and Ayurveda. He leads mindfulness, yoga, and productivity programs at businesses and yoga centers around the country, and yes, he would love to keynote your annual meeting or event. Brian lives in Northampton, Massachusetts, with his wife and his two sons. Learn more or reach out to him at www.teacherappears.net.

Matthew Oestreicher is a producer, performer, writer, an educator, and the author of the *Be You Card Deck for Teens* with coauthor Brian Leaf. He is the arranger/keyboardist/guitarist for the world-famous Apollo Theater Amateur Night Band in New York City and can be seen on FOX's *Showtime at the Apollo*. He has provided music for many national television shows and frequently works on Broadway. He is certified as a yoga teacher, an Integral Tai Chi/Chi Gong teacher, and a massage therapist. Matt has a degree in philosophy from Tufts University and a degree in music from the New England Conservatory of Music. He is currently completing a master's degree in mental health counseling at New York University. Matt is available for private coaching sessions and large group talks. He can be found at www.mattoestreicher.com.